# *Fearless!*

# Fearless!

## An Exotic Dancer's Guide to Personal and Professional Success

# Kerri Walker

Legacy Projects

*Fearless! An Exotic Dancer's Guide to
Personal and Professional Success*

First Edition

Published in the United States of America

ISBN-13: 978-1548794897
ISBN-10: 1548794899

Cover and Interior design by Bruce Kluger

For every beautiful woman determined
to start a journey for herself…

For Mike, for reminding me
to finish what I started …

And for René, for reminding me
to stay focused and relevant.

CONTENTS

ii

# Introduction

When I was 23 years old, I spent a year working as a fille au pair—a glorified babysitter—in a small village on the side of the Jura Mountains in the Rhône-Alpes of France. I could open my door and be hiking a mountain trail within five minutes and in less than an hour I could be approaching the summit with a view of Geneva, Switzerland, and Mont Blanc.

During my initial exploration, with a beginner's French dictionary in hand, the first word I learned was *tournesol*, which means sunflower. I had studied French in high school and struggled to memorize vocabulary, but when I looked at this flower, I had an "Aha" moment and discovered that *tourner* means turn, and *sol* means earth. Living the language through the different logic of French and English was fascinating and became like magic for me.

Aside from the obligations of work, my life became

a scavenger hunt of discovering things I loved. On weekends, I woke up early to run around Lake Geneva with a group of runners who introduced me to the best races in the area. I constantly met new people, who would tell me about a language meet-up in Geneva, where I met more like-minded, adventurous people, got invites to more cool activities, and ate Swiss fondue. Luckily, I maintained a small belly, thanks to a steady diet of Gruyere cheese and bread.

That year abroad was like a dream, as nature and new experience can leave an everlasting effect on your brain and your soul, but I felt a strong disconnect with the rest of my life back home in the States. A big part of me remained on that mountain, and I constantly dreamed of going back to live in the Rhône-Alpes.

To pull that off, I would have to get a good job, save lots of money, find a place to live, get a visa, and eventually just go. It seemed like an overwhelming project and I often considered giving up, but that would have meant compromising the rest of my life to stay comfortable in the United States. I couldn't accept that. Deep inside, I knew that all I really wanted was to return to Europe, where I missed being part of a culture I identified with so organically that I felt I should have been born there. I missed feeling like every day was an adventure.

I had to get focused if I wanted to make my dream a reality. I would need to save money, which was the biggest intimidation factor I had to overcome. Time was passing, and as I approached my 28th birthday, I was still living with my parents and dreaming of the Swiss Alps. I didn't have a plan. So I went on Google one day and searched for how to make a lot of money.

CHAPTER ONE: **One Step Closer**

*"Ni\*\*a, you need to git up,*
*git out and git something,*
*Don't let the days of your life pass by…*
*How will you make it if you never even try."*
—OutKast, "Git Up, Git Out"

I'm 30 now, and I've been stripping for three years.

A lot of us oversimplify what we haven't been exposed to and most people do that when it comes to how they perceive strippers—who they are and how they live their lives. Having an open mindset starts with good dialogue, and that's what I hope to provide for you.

For me, a change in mindset began with that Google search. While babysitting one day, I used the child's naptime to call a club and ask if they were hiring. They asked me to try out the next day. I told my parents I had another babysitting gig and drove anxiously down the

Garden State Parkway to a place called Layla's Lounge, about 40 miles away.

I was living with my parents at the time, which I had done on and off in my 20's while in between jobs and going to school. I had started my master's degree in French but had to stop after accruing $20,000 worth of debt in less than a year. I am not the most frugal person—I admit that—but I had no idea how expensive earning a graduate degree could be. I was an editor at a magazine for a little over a year but I hated the job and it didn't pay well, either. In fact, I was relieved when I got fired. It was hard living with my parents, even for just months at a time, but the Jersey Shore town they lived in was gorgeous, and conducive to lazy days at the beach.

As I drove down the highway to that club, I felt anxious but determined to learn what I needed in order to start working there right away and start making real money.

When I arrived, I found a dingy hole in the wall on the side of a roadway near a Wawa convenience store, which is about the most commonplace Jersey landmark there is. It was a couple months after summer, smack in the middle of the dead season, when the Jersey Shore clears out and people leave their summer homes and go back to New York City. Kids are back in school and it's just the locals and some commuters who are left to roam the strip malls and strip joints—not an exciting place to be unless you're in pursuit of money and a dream.

I told myself that getting there was half the battle, and since I'd done that I already felt better. That was the toughest part of the whole process—just getting there. That's what I encountered when I ran 5K races or marathons. Once you woke up, got dressed, and reached the starting line, the hardest part was over because the rest was just a matter of momentum. That was my mantra as I stepped inside the club, greeted the bouncer, and told him I was there to try out. He was as nice as can be, and I would later learn that bouncers are nice to you because you are a stripper with money. In this case, he knew right away that I would probably be dancing there so he let me in and showed me a seat.

It was the middle of the day in November and even though the club seemed almost empty I didn't fit in at all, but I'm usually a misfit so that didn't bother me. The weird thing was right away—I didn't know where to look. I didn't want to stare at the customers. They were so sad looking, tired, and overworked, a small bunch of blue-collar New Jersey guys on their lunch break, getting their thrill for the day.

After about two minutes of absolute shock ("What am I doing here?"), I flipped back into "achieving my goal" mode. I decided to look at the two naked girls on stage. One girl was tall, blonde, tan, and looked like a model. She was doing floor work on the stage. (Floor work is a category of dance movements in which more than just your feet are in contact with the floor. It is performed on stage and often gives dancers a rest from performing tricks and dancing on the pole.) She was spreading her legs, pointing her toes and pretending to touch herself—and getting tipped only a dollar at a time.

I was angry she wasn't getting more. I wanted to yell at those lousy guys who were so conservative with their tipping.

The other girl was stocky and pale, and had her brown frizzy hair pulled tightly back into a bun. She was loud and talkative and kept interacting with a customer sitting near me in a really nonchalant way, totally comfortable talking and being completely nude and putting herself in sexy positions on stage.

I sat and watched and immediately tried to learn what they were doing, what they were wearing (just heels), and how they interacted with the customers. I tried to absorb everything because I knew that I would be doing this very soon. When I was comfortable enough, I took the next step. I went to the stage and talked to the dancer with brown hair. I figured she was already talking a lot so why not add myself into the conversation?

> **Me:** Hey, how are you? I'm gonna try out. I've never stripped before in my life. This is the first time I've ever even been in a strip club. Are tryouts hard? *[Since I started stripping, I've stopped asking subjective questions, but that day I did.]*
>
> **Her:** It's so easy. I used to work in restaurants, I make more money here and it's so much easier. You make at least two hundred dollars cash when yah here, at least that.
>
> **Me:** Okay, that's awesome, but what about lap dances? What do I have to do?
>
> **Her:** You can do whateva you want. It's just a dance. You just hafta take your customer to the lap dance room and ya get fifteen bucks for every dance you give 'em. You pay the club five dollars for every dance. It's so easy.
>
> **Me:** So I make forty-five dollars for three dances?
>
> **Her:** Yep. *[She was still naked on stage the whole time we were talking.]* You've never been to a strip club before or worked in one?
>
> **Me:** Nope, never.
>
> **Her:** Wow, you're super brave to go right to a nude club.
>
> **Me:** Huh? People usually go to other ones?

**Her:** Well yeah, usually girls start at one where ya keep yer panties on.

**Me:** Okay, well as long as I'm safe. It's safe here, right?

**Her:** Yeah.

**Me:** I heard it was, that's why I chose this club.

**Her:** Yeah, you don't need to worry about that. Our bouncers walk you to your car at night. Don't worry, baby, you'll be fine.

**Me:** Thanks. What's your name?

**Her:** Amy.

**Me:** Cool, thanks.

Amy put my nerves at ease with her words but her demeanor and style of speaking stressed me out. She seemed so uneducated. I just concentrated on her advice. Outside of a strip club, I would never ask this girl for anything, but I had so many questions spinning in my head.

*How would I have the nerve to call someone I didn't know "baby"?*

*Will I be safe in a nude strip club?*

*What is this girl's idea of safe?*

I had so much to learn.

After we talked, Amy went to get the manager, who took me to his office. I was scared to be alone with him there. He took my driver's license, told me to get changed, and gave me directions for my audition.

It was hard to take him seriously and not laugh at him. He was wearing a Cosby sweater and glasses from the 1980's. His haircut was a subtle but noticeable high-top fade and he had an overly groomed moustache. To me, he looked like a strip club manager.

"Did you give the DJ two songs you want?"

"No, not yet."

"Okay, after you get changed tell him two songs

you want to dance to. They can be anything you want. And you know what to wear?"

"Yes, I have a small bikini and heels."

"Okay, put those on in the changing room."

"Is there a locker for my stuff?"

"No, I promise it will be fine. My girls don't steal. Just don't bring anything too valuable. So go get changed and talk to the DJ, and on the first song you have to take your top and bottom off."

At the time, I was very low maintenance when it came to wearing makeup or straightening my hair. Since college, I had always been confident in my looks. I liked being as close to natural as possible and I never wore a lot of makeup, if any at all, and I liked to leave my hair alone and keep away from chemical products or heat.

I don't want to sound like your mother, but trust your looks!

A few minutes later, I emerged wearing a cheap pair of heels from Marshall's and a two-piece bikini that I bought at a sex shop. I learned later that week to buy Pleaser heels from a sex shop or Amazon. They are made for strippers, and in my opinion Pleaser makes the best, most comfortable, and cutest stripper heels.

I told the DJ what songs I wanted. He was pleasant enough but his eyes never left my body to look at my face when I was speaking. I went on stage, danced, and got naked to a Pearl Jam song, and then one by Beyonce. It had been easy for me to get naked on stage. The butterflies in my stomach went away as soon as I got into the groove of the music.

When I came off stage, I was told I had a job.

I changed back right away into my street clothes. As I drove up the Garden State Parkway to my parents' house, I knew that living with my parents while stripping would be way too weird so I quickly arranged to rent a room from a woman I knew from my gym.

For the next few days before moving, I hid my dancing clothes in the trunk of my car and kept quiet about my new employment. My parents and I never spoke much anyway, so nothing really changed. Within a week, I was gone and paying $400 a month for some privacy.

On my next ride back to the club, I was alone with some really weird feelings about what I was getting into, but one thing was clear: I was one step closer to my goal of moving to France.

CHAPTER TWO: **Eye on the Prize**

*"To get where you wanna be,
you have to set a goal,
and keep your eyes on the prize."*
    —Marley Marl, "Keep Your Eyes on the Prize"

I felt numb for the first couple days at the club, as everything seemed so surreal—the girls, the managers, and the customers—I couldn't level with anyone. I didn't want to smoke or drink with the girls in the back room. I didn't want to chat with the managers, and I spoke with the customers only to get their money. I preferred remaining in my own world, where I could maintain focus, because I was there solely to make money, not to socialize with anyone.

Thanksgiving marked my third day of work, and I was already making more in a single day than I had ever made in my life.

I knew that in order to keep that up I had to avoid distractions. A lot of the dancers spent time in the back room, smoking, drinking, and talking. They were either mean to me or asked me to spend more time with them, and neither one was appealing. I didn't talk much to the girls who were nice to me, and didn't get upset with the ones who were mean, even those who did their fair share of bullying. I never considered the club to be a sorority or anything like that. In fact, I capitalized on the girls hanging out in the back room because that meant fewer of them on the dance floor where the customers—and the money—were.

The club was full of rough girls. Some were doing hard drugs; some had babies too young, and some had boyfriends and baby daddies in jail. Many were undereducated and could barely read. When I went back to the changing room to use the bathroom, get a drink of water, or take a break, I heard their stories and telephone conversations. Overall, they were pretty bad. One girl, Cassie, was HIV positive and an alcoholic.

A dancer doesn't go around telling you her vices. You find them out by being around them and observing their behavior. Amy had a boyfriend in jail. She was planning how she wanted to do her probation—get it all done in one shot, or spread it out over time. This was a common topic of conversation in the back room.

The beautiful, tall blonde I saw the day I came in to try out, Kitty, was usually passed out in the changing room, mid-cigarette, because she was so constantly high on painkillers.

Then there was Lucy—a young mommy 18 years old—tall, lean, and tan, with long, brown, curly hair. She looked like a Victoria's Secret model. She was drunk every time I worked with her. I didn't like to talk to her because I wanted to fix her.

"Lucy," I said to her one day, "why don't you try modeling in New York City? You have the perfect body and face for it. I could easily see you in a magazine. Plus, you're the perfect age to do it."

"No," she said, giggling. She was always laughing. "I like it here, and I don't want to be told what to do. That would suck."

I left it at that.

One girl always had a book in front of her, as she was studying to be a nurse. Another was a friend of a friend from a nice town and family. She was a young mom, simply dancing for the money. Another beautiful girl who looked like a model drove all the way from the city to New Jersey to dance. She was in law school. Her dad was a cop in Manhattan, so she needed to avoid being seen by anyone he might know. Another girl had a master's degree in journalism from NYU. She was dancing to pay back her student loans. I'd already paid back almost $20K in student debt from my aborted master's degree so the money I was making at the club was all going for one thing—getting back to France.

I wished I could have turned back the hands of time and quit college years ago to become a stripper. It seemed like it would have been more fun to do it at a younger age instead of going to college, especially if it also included focusing on long-term goals. For example, had I danced from the age of 19 to 22, I could have lived independently, saved money, and learned about subjects in real-life and gone back to school later—more motivated to learn what I really wanted. I started out in college as an economics major. At that time, I did not even own a debit card and certainly didn't have any money to invest. But as a dancer, I was handling my own finances, investing money in stocks and mutual funds, and reading The New York Times business section. I developed a genuine understanding of economics. I could have learned that in real life and also had money saved to go back to school in my mid-to late twenties. By going to college right after high school, I was not as motivated to learn about subjects that seemed so abstract and foreign to me.

## Find Your Oasis

That first week I danced at the strip club while still living at my parents' house was a nightmare. Most parents would hate the idea of their daughter working at a strip club and I felt terrible about that. I know dancers whose parents are cool with them in that profession. Obviously, it takes an open-minded type of person to understand, but I was all but certain that wasn't my folks, or most others, for that matter.

You are dancing to jumpstart your financial nest egg and bring you closer to your long-term goal. But it makes no sense to stay at mom and dad's house to save money because you will make enough to save and live on your own. Plus, the job will be stressful enough without adding those types of complications.

When I moved in with the woman I had met at the gym she knew I was starting out as a dancer and I was so grateful she was open-minded enough to rent to me despite my job, and even had faith in me being successful. Her boyfriend thought I was a bartender, which is funny because I have no knowledge at all of mixed drinks.

I like speaking my mind, so it was great opening up to her about stripping. But at the same time, she asked so many questions about my job. This was exhausting. The last thing I wanted to do in my free time was answer questions about my work. If more people knew what I really did, they would ask me questions all the time.

Stripping peaks people's curiosity. It's important to keep your boundaries. After living with this woman for six months, and avoiding becoming her friend because I needed my own space to relax when I wasn't working, I knew it was time to move on.

I may have seemed like a total bitch, but I thought I would rather be a bitch and go for my goals than to do things just to have a reputation for being nice. I had to move. She wanted a friend and I just wanted my space.

### What About Family?

As long as I danced, I never told my parents or my two older brothers what I was doing.

"I'm a freelance editor," I said to my dad one night when we were out for pizza. I'd been dancing already for quite some time. We had never talked much when I was growing up and it was weird to be out to dinner with him, just the two of us. He showed me a picture of a new, beautiful house my brother had just bought and casually suggested he would be okay with me dating an older man—a topic I definitely did *not* bring up. We were so painfully disconnected from each other.

Those were the days I still called and texted my parents. Eventually, I stayed in contact with them through email, and even that was a struggle, as their life was a soap opera of dad cheating on my mom (again) and his emails, asking to see me immediately to make amends as part of a 12-step program.

I loved my family, but I had to stop talking to them because it became the only way to protect myself from verbal abuse. They were never far from me geographically, but both my brothers and my dad held busy, high-stress jobs in finance. Over the years I came to feel more and more disconnected from them. My mom was always either too preoccupied with running errands or just too unhappy. We never had a mother-daughter connection. I walked on eggshells around my family, especially with my parents. Even growing up, my feelings were not valued, and when I was going through normal hormonal changes I was forced to go to a psychiatrist and take bipolar medication—at the age of 14! Even as I became an adult living on my own, my mom was still trying to diagnose me and tell me things that were wrong with me.

In college, when my dad cheated on my mom, she blamed me, saying I caused them too much stress when I was in high school. I guess sending me away to a boarding school created a financial strain, but there's no good enough justification for verbal abuse and manipulation.

My dad cheated on my mom again after I became a dancer. The same things happened again, even when I was out of their life. They were still unhappy, but I wasn't around to be blamed or verbally abused, not anymore. For me, it was easy not to talk to my family while I was a dancer. I still loved them and told them in emails, but otherwise, I had to create boundaries for my own sanity.

## Taking Care of You
I don't want to sound like your mother (here I go again), but take care of *you*!

When I first moved to New York, I had roommates, but none of them knew what I did for a living. I found it difficult sharing a space, even though I loved saving the money. Eventually, I rented a studio. I moved twice in less than a year. Since dancers are paid cash, it is hard to rent a place without roommates. A lot of landlords want to see a W2. I finally found one who did not require any paperwork.

Your club should be able to write you a letter that states your yearly income. It should have a letterhead with the club's name. They can say that you are a hostess. Ask your manager for one if you need it.

I found my new home in Astoria, Queens, through a realtor. I had saved enough money for the first month's rent, a small realtor's fee, a security deposit, and movers. Moving can be a lot of work in New York City.

"Let's toast to the fact that I've moved out of my mama's basement," says Drake, "to a condo downtown, 'cause it's 'all about location.'"

He's right. My studio became my oasis when I wasn't working.

CHAPTER THREE: **Rules of the Road**

*"Look way deep inside yourself,*
*Discover the diamond inside,*
*find ya wealth."*
    —Nas, "Find Ya Wealth"

**Rule #1:** *Be beautiful, inside and out.*

That means don't do drugs and don't drink.

I don't want to sound like your mother (I know), but in these types of work settings it's so easy to drink and you will easily drink too much without meaning to if you allow yourself. You're exposed to it every day. There are so many horror stories of drugs and drinking to the point of addiction or death over the course of working at a strip club.

Girls who drink, do drugs, and get into prostitution for more money outside the club usually continue on a downward spiral.

I worked in New York City with a 23-year-old dancer named Hope, who was always high on OxyContin. She was physically beautiful, a sporty-looking Dominican girl from the Bronx, with an incredible body, and seemed full of potential, but her life was spinning out of control right in front of us. Besides drugs, she had a devastating spending habit and constantly blew money on clothes, hair, vacations, and expensive restaurants. She stole from other dancers, too. We all knew it was Hope when something went missing. She broke into some of the girls' lockers and took whatever she could. When she was working at a different club—after she was fired from ours—she went home with a dancer after work and stayed up all night doing coke with her. When her coworker finally passed out, Hope robbed her of $2,000 in cash and a gun. I heard she ended up in jail for having another girl killed.

Another girl I worked with on and off for a couple months was Kirsten, a gorgeous woman, 33 years old, half-Irish and half-Japanese, who had worked in the sex industry since she was 18. Before that, she had been a professionally trained ballerina in New York City. She wore a tight, neat bun, and her frame was strong and lean like a ballerina's, but over time, it had whittled down more and more. It was easy to see what bothered her. Kirsten had a brother addicted to heroin and a mom who wanted her support, and she was feeling too old to continue stripping. She drank, and took way too many Xanax. She was very funny, but also quite sarcastic, to the point of being defensive and negative.

One morning at work, Kirsten had mixed pills with alcohol, and she passed out in my arms while we were talking to a customer. I felt her chest and thought that her heart was going to come right out of her chest. It seemed like straight out of a cartoon when one of the characters falls in love and his heart literally beats out of his chest. I kept her number on my phone to check up on her once in a while to see if she was still alive, but weeks passed without hearing from her and I never saw or heard from her again.

**Rule #2:** *Stay focused on your goals.*

One night of reckless behavior could turn deadly.

The reason you are stripping is not to party to excess but to get in and get out—unscathed and with your financial goals met. You will make a lot of money. You do not need to do drugs or drink.

In fact, I recommend not drinking at all on the job because it is too easy to grow accustomed to knocking back a few every night. A lot of customers come in every night. Some guys are gentlemen and will respect your wishes not to drink. Others will be pushy. They are looking for a drinking partner or they want you drunk because they figure this will eventually make you "easy."

Be confident enough to stick to your guns and say no—more than once, if necessary—and the customer will either forget that you are not drinking and he is, or he will not get dances from you and you will have to walk away. He will eventually get a different girl.

**Rule #3:** *It's okay to lose a customer.*

If a guy will only go to a private room with you if you agree to do a sexual favor or to do drugs or drink, then *do not go.* With some men, you can get them in a room by saying, "Come on, we'll have such a sexy time, better than out here on the dance floor." This works to get some men in the private rooms. But some men have been coming to strip clubs for years and they want to know for sure that when they are in a private room you will be doing "what they paid for." So they won't go unless you say, "I will drink or I will do coke or I will have sex." Get away from this customer. If an undercover cop hears you promise this to a customer, you could be arrested. If your manager knows you said this, and you do not comply with what you said, then the manager may not pay you for your room. This might happen if the room ends early. Just save yourself the headache. Walk away. The worst thing you can do is drinking, drugs, or sex.

Your self-esteem and health are more important. When you drink and do drugs, it negatively affects your appearance—inside the club and out. You will age much faster. Be aware of your body. It's the only one you have!

**Rule #4:** *Looks are important, but don't become obsessive.*
It's fun to look good, and when you get that together it will make you feel good, too. But putting too much pressure on your outside appearance can cause lots of stress. First and foremost, establish and maintain good nutrition (Chapter 8), exercise, and keep your priorities straight!

I don't want to sound like your mother (relax), but make sure you have paper towels in your house before you go buy the latest Chanel bag.

Be glamorous if that makes you happy. If you like spending your money on hair extensions, fake nails, and tons of makeup, go for it, but only as long as you can stick to your budget.

"Cause everything designer, her jeans is Helmut Lang/Shoes is Alexander Wang and her shirt the newest Donna Karan, wearing all the Cartier frames/Jean Paul Gaultier's 'cause they match with her persona."

Remember: Those lyrics from "Fashion Killa" by A$AP Rocky are from a song, not your life.

Be patient. Some girls enjoy being beauty queens on the street, and they look like strippers even when you run into them outside the club. On the other hand, some strippers, myself included, look like your average girl next door—someone you would never guess in a million years was working in a strip club at night.

I didn't change my look too much when I went to work. I had stripper heels, a dress, a thong, and makeup, which was already way outside my usual comfort zone. I didn't need to add to it during my off hours. But if you want to be professional at what you do, there are a few things you have to take care of because they will make a real difference in your success.

**Rule #5:** *Hair and makeup are super-important.*

If your club has a makeup artist, use them, and tip them well. Our makeup artists let us pick what look we wanted. Every night when it was my turn, it was the same routine.

"Okay, sit down," they'd say. "What are we doing tonight?"

We had two makeup artists, Gabriel and Mateo, and each had different personalities. Mateo was more Nars, using lots of bright colors. Gabriel was more Bobby Brown, smoky eyes, and conservative. They were both geniuses at details, like contouring, highlighting, and blending.

They made it fun to sit in their chair. I joked with Gabriel that he was my therapist. He invited me to come in early to work to teach me how to do my eyes, and I learned from him. Even girls who were good at doing their own makeup sat with the artists because they provided a different look than what they usually did.

"Our job is to give girls the best face so that they can make the most money," said Mateo.

It's a physical and emotional transformation for most girls. I was Kerri during the day, but when my dress was on and my makeup was done, I became Mica.

**Rule #6:** *Safety trumps everything.*

My first time working at Layla's was a mandatory day shift. I arrived in my piece-of-shit silver 2004 Chevy

Malibu at 11:30 in the morning. My shift would start an hour later. I soon discovered that it was a bad idea to be so punctual.

I popped my trunk and got out of my car. I grabbed a bag with my heels and the one outfit I owned, along with a jug of water. I walked to the door I had entered the day I'd auditioned and found it locked. I knocked. No answer. There were no windows to peer into, so I had no clue if anyone was there. I went back to my car, locked the door, and waited for someone to open the club so I could get ready. I guess I was dumb not to drive next door to the Wawa and wait there, but who knew?

A man who seemed high out of his mind on something came running over and knocked on my window. I screamed. Brad—I would learn his name later that day when I gave him a lap dance—was a punctual customer who was desperately waiting for the club to open. I didn't know what he wanted when he lunged at my car, and I was scared, so I did the dumbest thing I could. I hid under my steering wheel and waited for him to go away. Thank God, he actually did, and I saw him back in his car, waiting for the club to open. I stayed in my car until Brad and I eventually were let into the club.

*Always be aware of your surroundings.*

*Don't ever be alone, even in the daytime.*

Daytime is when the nastiest customers come out and the raunchiest girls are working at the club. Prestige does exist in stripping. A night shift is superior to a day shift. My next shift would be at night. It was kind of like being promoted.

I suggest you go to a club and learn about it before you consider working there. The dancers and bouncers at Layla's told me that I would be safe there, and that a bouncer would walk me to my car at night. I had nothing to compare the club to, and was really worried about my safety, as I knew it had to be my biggest priority.

Six months after I began stripping in New Jersey, I moved to New York City. I bought an unlimited, monthly subway pass, which saved me money. When I went to the club I was tempted to take the subway both ways to avoid spending money on a taxi. I waited for a coworker, or even better, a group of coworkers, to go with me. If it was a crowded Saturday morning, I took the subway by myself. If it was a desolate Monday morning, I took a taxi alone or the subway with coworkers. It all came down to respecting myself. I never allowed myself to get desensitized to my surroundings, and I carried pepper spray.

Personally, I felt safer commuting home by subway or taxi instead of driving alone in my car through suburban New Jersey. I had often heard of girls being followed home by clients, so for the first six months I always checked my rearview mirror. After all, I was driving home pretty tired some nights, and it probably would have been easy for someone to follow me and not have me notice. In the end, I found it much safer to be a dancer in a big city.

**Rule #7:** *Manage your managers.*

Club managers are not horrible people as long as you don't spend too much time with them. Of course, some are much more professional than others. I'll talk about the unprofessional ones. If they are in a good mood, they will pretend to be your buddy and your best pal. The less you share with them about your personal life and your schedule outside of work, the better off you will be. For example, it is not a good idea to tell them that you can't work next week because you'll be skiing in Colorado. This kind of information will probably be used against you later on when you want to take another holiday. Keep your answers short, and be confident, or you will become their puppet.

A typical interchange should go like this:

> **Manager:** I need you to make your schedule
> for next week.
> **Dancer:** I'll do Monday to Wednesday.
> **Manager:** I need you to work either Friday
> or Saturday next week.
> **Dancer:** I can only give you Monday to
> Wednesday. I'm so sorry. It's all I can do.
> **Manager:** I can't have you keep giving me
> half a schedule. Must be nice. I don't take
> that sort of time off.

That's how the conversation ends. Smile, shrug, and move on. Done. Let the nervous feelings in your stomach settle, and no matter what, do not feed the manager empty words. It is not your job to keep him satisfied 100 percent of the time.

Of course, another thing to keep in mind is that managers will try to break boundaries with you, but in a smart, playful way. They sincerely want to fuck the brains out of their dancers, but they won't unless you comply.

Their first priority is collecting money and running the club. But they will try to get in your panties and will never stop trying. Remember, even if you are alone with the manager in his office and you are half naked, you are still safe. They will treat you just well enough so that you come back to work there. Nothing more. Nothing less.

Don't forget, too, that you give the club money to work there each night.

Managers are people, too. They have family lives and pressure from the club owners to collect money. They are real men surrounded by naked women, who are just doing their job.

The dancer-manager relationship is a delicate balance of power that you have to continuously uphold. Don't be afraid when managers make passes at you. If they touch your leg, that's all that happened, so let it go. Say no in a flirtatious way, and it's done. Don't get emotional. Flirting makes them feel more powerful in front of the other men at the club who have to pay to touch the girls. A manager has earned the right to display a certain perk that he can touch and flirt with the dancers—without paying. It's part of their job and probably their innate personality.

If they are really attracted to you, then their effort to get you to fuck them will be stronger and you will have to reciprocate in an unemotional, matter-of-fact yet playful way, with a firm attitude, by saying something such as, "I'm here to work" or "Sorry, never on the job." Maintain a tough mindset and let some things go. Sexual harassment is an unfortunate part of the job. Just say no and they should not escalate. Otherwise, find a new club.

**Rule #8:** *Learn to cope with bullying.*
Even if I worked 365 nights a year, paid my house fee (see Glossary) every night, always came to work on time, and tipped people once in a while—in other words, even if I was the perfect employee, I'm pretty sure I still would have gotten yelled at by my first manager in New York City.

I suppose I was vulnerable because I was sweet and not terribly confident when I first started working at that club in Times Square. The manager preyed on girls like that. Plus, since I worked at the same one for my first two years in the city, he figured I would not go anywhere, which he thought gave him license to really yell at me, which he did all the time.

He would yell at me for things like sitting with customers before the waitress came over to take drink orders, which he made up, as I did not do that, or when

I told new girls not to sit with customers before the waitress came. He told me to be a team player with the new girls and not to bully them, or he'd yell at me for letting guys touch me during dances, which was also bullshit because every girl got touched during dances. I always made a successful effort to get touched less during dances.

Also, when I cashed out my "funny money" (more on that in Chapter 6) at the end of the night, he would only do some of it at a time. I think this happened to all of the girls, but it happened to me the most. I had started out tipping him once a week, just because I thought it was a nice thing to do. When I stopped tipping him, I noticed he was not as pleasant to work with. One night, when I wasn't feeling well, I went home early (two hours after I'd arrived) and he did not return my $140 house fee. I didn't want to deal with him and didn't ask for it back.

I was one of the nicest and well-behaved dancers at our club and was never late for a shift and never skipped any, either. What he accused me of was always complete bullshit. I often went out of my way to help girls I liked make money. I waited longer than other dancers for customers to get their drinks. I'm pretty sure the manager tried to play mind games with me by yelling at me for things that were not true. He did it when I stepped on the toes of girls who made a lot of money and tipped the club well, or when I told new girls when they were not following the rules and stepping on my toes.

Honestly, I felt sick when that bastard yelled at me. Other dancers and the host, all of whom I had worked with for about two years by that point, told me the same thing when I confided in them—that he was bullying me.

They had no shortage of advice:

"Don't worry about it."

"He is a miserable human being."

"I've seen him be a lot worse with other girls."

"Just ignore it."

"Try another club."

"If you work sometimes at another club, than he knows you could possibly leave if he doesn't stop yelling at you. This might make him stop."

"The managers just had a meeting about enforcing some of the rules. That's why he's yelling about it."

"Just stay calm and it'll stop."

All these comments gave me ideas of what I could do.

I eventually got out of my routine comfort zone and went to work at a different club in Times Square about five blocks away. It was such a good move for me. I felt confident from the beginning, made more money right away, and had a fresh start with the managers and other girls. I went back to the old club once in a while when I knew the nicer manager was working, but I didn't rely on it like I once did.

I regret not dancing at different clubs sooner than I did. I became happier and less stressed. If a manager or another dancer were bullying me, I could "escape" to work at another club and come back on my own terms. There are so many places to dance just within the 10 square blocks that make up Times Square. By literally walking away from one club to work at another, I wasn't walking away from dancing altogether, just from that one club.

**Rule #9:** *Keep it to yourself.*

I recommend not sharing with anyone that you are a stripper. I only told my accountant because I had to, and I told a few of my closest friends. I told most people that I was an editor. If you do decide to tell someone, especially someone who might not know much about dancing, then be ready to answer a lot of questions or to be judged harshly.

**Rule #10:** *Get straight with the dating game.*

Dating can be especially tricky. A lot of the girls I worked with who were dating did not tell that they were a stripper, at least not in the beginning of the relationship. The beginning of a relationship was usually considered the first couple of months. I saw a trend with dancers from my club who were dating that their relationships didn't get past those first couple of months. Relationships don't last (in my opinion) if you aren't able to be open about what you do. I tried dating while I was dancing, and I found my dates were pretty boring. I was working four to five times a week and I could not talk about work. I couldn't talk about a big part of my life and I avoided questions about anything work related. I told guys I was a cocktail waitress, but I didn't want to talk about it. If I was on a date and got asked about being a waitress, I gave short answer lies. It always sounded like I was hiding something. My schedule was not conducive to dating, either.

If you do tell a potential boyfriend or a guy you just met that you are a stripper, then there is definitely a chance he will want you only because many men have a weird fantasy about dating a stripper. In my opinion, the best options are: you can choose to date and tell potential boyfriends that you are a dancer and from there you can weed out the good from the bad, or you can choose not to date while you are a dancer. It's a choice.

CHAPTER FOUR: **Owning Your Identity**

*"What's your real name?*
*And not your stripper name.*
*I make it rain on ya, like a windowpane."*
  —Juicy J, "Bandz a Make Her Dance"

"So what's your name?"

When you first become a stripper you *have* to pick a stage name, which is not that big of a deal. Of course, you could use your real name, but more than likely it's not as fun or exotic as the new name you will choose.

It will become second nature pretty quickly, too. I got so accustomed to using my stage name when I was working four or five times a week that I mistakenly introduced myself as my stripper name in real life—more than once, for sure. This is okay. When you do, just make a quick unnoticeable recovery or simply laugh off your slip up.

Once you pick your name, it's hard to change it. It's what other dancers at your club will call you forever, and that's how they'll refer to you with the customers, too.

I picked my stripper name before I started working. I chose "Mata," after Mata Hari. I thought it was a great choice because Mata Hari, born in the Netherlands in 1876, was a professional exotic dancer who also became a spy for France in 1916. Soon after, Mata Hari was accused of spying for Germany, as well, and she was executed in 1917 after being exposed as a double agent.

It turns out that using that name was cool until practically every conversation I had with customers turned into me providing a repetitive history lesson for my uninformed male guests.

Keep in mind that only an idiot will ask you for your real name. This is usually a good indicator to move on to a different customer. A good way to possibly avoid this is picking a realistic dancer name, such as Lily or Emma, unless your name is Lily or Emma.

When I changed clubs from the Jersey Shore to Times Square in New York City, I chose Mica. Minerals make popular stripper names, such as Sapphire, Diamond, and Candy, and cities work, too, such as Paris, London, or Sydney.

Don't overthink your name. It's a job. It's not your whole life.

**Keeping a Grip**
Stripping can be lonely. Working nights and sleeping until one in the afternoon can get you seriously feeling like you're living in a different dimension. Besides working nights, you will probably work Fridays and/or Saturdays, too, as well as covering some holidays, which is expected in most clubs.

Kid Cudi says it: "It's crazy, But all along, All along, I

knew I was meant to be alone, Out there on my own, yeah."

That sucks. Being in a strip club on a major holiday can be pretty depressing.

I lost contact with what I consider the normal people of the daytime world, the ones who wake up at six or seven in the morning to be at work on time by nine and end their day by five or six. Usually I was going home from work about two or three hours before rush hour. At some point during my first year of dancing, I gave up on being normal and let the stripper time dimension take over.

This is another reason that stripping should be a temporary job—a few years and then out, because it is not healthy to sustain this lifestyle for too long. It's better not to get too sucked in to this lonely world, as it could cause depression. Of course many people work night shifts in their careers, but I was not telling many people about what I did for a living, and that kind of mindset can get lonely.

It is easy as a lone wolf personality type or a social personality type to get sucked in to the temptations of free time that dancing gives you. I don't mean to sound like a mom, but use your free time to connect to society how you truly want to. Look for an internship, travel, write a book, gain a skill, or take classes, even if it's once a week or taking a trip once a month, because staying connected to society outside of the strip club will help keep you sane.

I liked that I could pass the day with the freedom to go to the gym when I pleased or read a book or go for a walk. But I also made sure to connect, to travel with friends, and to do volunteer work with other people. I could have easily passed my days alone but I forced myself not to. I had so much freedom to do what I wanted during the day.

CHAPTER FIVE: **The Shark Tank**

*"That don't kill me, can only make me stronger."*
—Kanye West, "Stronger"

Velvet, the New York City club, was a lot more complex than Layla's. In New Jersey, I was on an island and did not have to talk much with the other girls. But in New York, the girls went after customers like sharks. We all pretty much stayed on the floor from eight p.m. till four a.m. That meant steady contact with the other dancers and no break from the customers. Intense! And it added a lot of complexity to the job when it came to relationships.

A lot of girls were short-timers, working anywhere from a few days to a few weeks. Many were beautiful, with great personalities, and worked really hard. But if they didn't make as much money as they had expected to make, it was because they hadn't established working relationships with the managers and bouncers, as well as with the other dancers.

In short, they didn't take the time to figure out the scene and how to make it work for them.

Our core group of girls, including me, stayed for years. The longer we remained, the more we flowed together. We got used to each other and to the idiosyncrasies of our club. We often pulled each other over to do double lap dances. Or, if we danced for a guy and didn't tell him we did two, we could keep a poker face together. It was like we could communicate without using words to keep calm and stand by our assertions. Girls I worked with for years knew not to sit next to each other when we waited for customers to come in and be seated. I could also ask dancers I knew to cash out my money for me if I was busy.

Stripping in New York City is popular with girls from Russia, Eastern Europe, and Spanish-speaking countries, and at Velvet, that meant adapting to a whole lot of new cultures and lifestyles. In order to succeed, I had to learn about working with people who had different backgrounds and views on life.

### Candy

Candy was a Dominican woman who spoke very little English. At first, I couldn't stand the sight of her. She was about 60 pounds heavier than me, about half a foot shorter, and carried most of her weight in her ass. She often did lap dances for a customer without asking if they wanted one or explaining that it costs money.

One of my first encounters with Candy happened at about 3:30 in the morning on a painfully slow night, when a group of guys sat down and Candy and I moved—much like cheetahs chasing prey on the safari—across the floor as quickly as possible to sit with them before any of the other dancers could. One guy wanted infinite lap dances at $20 a song until the club closed. Not surprisingly, he was the drunkest and most vulnerable one of the group. The other two guys wanted beer. Since I was in closer proximity to the guy who wanted those dances, I figured I was entitled to dance for him, but Candy cut right in front of me and started dancing for him.

At the time, I was a new dancer in the club.

"No way," I said, "Go dance for someone else."

Candy looked at me—she had the eye of the tiger that night—and slapped me on the leg. No one had ever done that to me before, for any reason—ever. I was pissed. I went to the manager and used my best matter-of-fact voice to sound as cool as possible.

"Lucky just slapped me."

I always mixed up everyone's names when I was new. The manager ignored me and did absolutely nothing.

For some time after this incident, Candy and I didn't talk. But time made things better. It was too uncomfortable for us to hold a grudge, not when we were working together four or five nights a week.

All the dancers and managers knew how she worked. Even though her behavior was not fair, everyone looked the other way. Sometimes things go on like that and you just have to accept them. I don't think Candy tipped anyone in our club, but she was able to get away with things that other girls could not. Maybe everyone just knew that it was the only way she could survive and make any money. She was older, did not speak English, and she was not "beautiful."

So while managers looked the other way for Candy when she didn't follow basic rules of the club, they also let things slide with girls who tipped well and gave the new girls some slack—at least for a little while.

Unless you are brand new to a club, managers don't want to hear you complain. It is best just to adapt to all the unfairness you may see going on around you. After some time working in New York City, I had the same response whenever girls complained to me about unfair management and how the club was being run.

"What are you going to do?" I said. "Change the system? Argue with the managers and owners of our club? For all we know, they could be part of the Mafia."

I said this to remind myself, too. I dealt with the unfairness and still made money.

## Brandy and Star

This creature was one of the few American dancers at our club in New York City. I affectionately called her Satan, while she called me Jesus. Our backgrounds were completely different. She started stripping when she was 18 years old and I started when I was 28. She had fully embraced being a stripper and was 31 when we met. I was still very tentative and learning the ropes in a very studious, cerebral way. She was fired after my first year because she had punched another dancer.

On the first day we met, she decided she liked me and wanted to help me by sprinkling me with stripper wisdom.

"Don't sell the private room to the customer or tell him the prices of the rooms," she told me on my first night. "Bring him to the host. The host does the sales. Your job is to dance and entertain."

Brandy knew I didn't do drugs or drink so she tailored her lectures and I learned how to make more money by observing how she worked, separating the drugs and alcohol from the good advice.

She had a hot partner that she worked with, an Irish girl named Star, with amazing fake boobs and a big butt and the best Irish brogue in the world. Often, when two girls work as partners, one is all personality and one is all looks.

In New York City, time is money, so when they talked to customers, Star and Brandy upsold themselves. This meant they asked for a lot of money on tips for private rooms, and they demanded to go to the most expensive one in the house. If they spent a lot of time talking to a guy, they sometimes asked him for tips on the floor, just for their time.

Star and Brandy drank with the customers. Then they would get them to want to do coke in a private room. Star hid the coke in her panties. She would discretely show it to the customer during the floor dances by sliding her panties to the side to reveal the bag of coke and then a little more—her pussy.

This was the bait to get a drunken guy into a private room, where things got out of control. They did coke and gave sexual favors. A one-hour private room at our club cost $1,100 for one girl and double for two. Each girl would get $500 and the house would get the rest. Tipping was optional, but highly encouraged by the girls and the host, and they added up to $200 to $500 dollars per hour, per girl.

On good nights, Brandy and Star could keep customers in private rooms all night. If they did more than dance, they tipped the manager working that night.

But what if you don't drink or do coke or give sexual favors?

"If you don't drink or do blow," said Brandy, "that's fine. Don't pretend you do. Just be real, 'cause that's what they want to see. Don't be an idiot and tell them where you live or where you hang out, but be real about your experience and what you're about so they can connect with you. Just make them feel like this fantasy is real."

I rarely kept guys in rooms all night. Usually it was

only Brandy and Star who did. But when I did get a guy to stay in a room for hours, it was because I had focused my energy to find a connection with that guy or because he was extremely intoxicated.

The floor was like Brandy and Star's chessboard. They were patient, waiting for the other dancers to make a wrong move with any rich customers. They did not give a lot of $20 dances on the floor. I would often see Brandy sitting and waiting and reading the floor. When the right customer arrived, she sensed it, and beelined to him.

Brandy and Star were almost always working two customers. Brandy would be with one and Star with another, since this would double their chances of getting into a private room. They signaled to each other from across the room how the conversation was going with their customers.

If Brandy or Star were called by the DJ to dance on stage, instead of leaving their customer on the floor, one of them would dance on stage in her place. They did this a lot. If only one of them were working that night, and the other couldn't fill in for them on stage, Brandy or Star would tip the cocktail waitress to tell the DJ to keep them off stage and the waitress would hand the DJ his tip. They pushed the rules and did not get punished. This was because they tipped. Everyone was happy, host and manager included.

Brandy was diplomatic toward all the dancers, but only during idle time, like in the dressing room when we were all getting dressed and doing our makeup and hair, or on the dance floor, when the club was empty of customers but full of dancers. Like a politician, she listened to everyone's problems, empathized, and gave advice. She was sincere, but it was also part of making money. Dancers remember you when you are nice to them.

She pulled me aside one day during a shift.

"You think I like these bitches?" she said.

She had noticed me being unresponsive to the other girls.

"I don't care about them," she said, "but I smile and I pretend to. It's all part of what we do."

Brandy gave me so much good advice when I was brand new. I loved her for all the help she offered. She's the one who told me to get an accountant and how to dance sexy. She made me feel comfortable when I was new. In turn, I helped her out many times, too. I gave her massages when the club was slow. I brought her to a private room with me a couple of times when my customers asked for another girl. But when the club got busy, when it was full of customers and dancers to compete with, Brandy's only focus was on making money, not on being empathetic or nice to the other dancers. She knew which dancers would be going on stage in what order, so she knew when to steal their customers. Often, she would sit close to a dancer who she knew was going to be called to dance onstage. Once the dancer was called up, she unapologetically would slide in to take that girl's customer.

I will never forget the night she did this to me. The bouncer sat a guy next to me. In our club, bouncers did that, while in other clubs they may not. It was obvious that this customer had money he wanted to spend. As soon as he sat next to me and after we introduced each other, he wanted dances. He even started asking me about the private rooms. He ordered drinks for both of us. I thought it would be an easy private room. But when I saw Brandy out of the corner of my eye, I knew it was all over. I didn't know the order of when the dancers were called to stage, but I knew she did and she was sitting close to me. She and Star were waiting like hawks. Sure enough, I was called to stage on the next song. My stomach dropped. For the first time in my stripper career since my first week, I was angry. I had to go on stage and dance for whatever I could get while they made thousands off of that guy in the private room.

## Getting Over the Guilt
In the beginning, I felt guilty trying to "drain" a man's bank account.

"If a man is out at the club," said Brandy, "he is there to spend money, so why not on you? If you don't get it, some other bitch will."

Brandy had no remorse and neither did Star. When they talked to a customer, they discretely observed how expensive his clothes were. Brandy was an expert in spotting a real Rolex versus a fake. She could smell expensive cologne and name the brand. She could identify designer shoes and knew about how much they cost. Besides what a customer was wearing, Brandy and Star found out about his career and what he owned. Once they found out a man had money, it was all over. They kept men coming back to see them at the club, again and again. It didn't matter if he was married with kids or going through a tough time in his life. If he had money, they were going to prey on him.

I remember being in the dressing room one night and changing into one of the three dresses I owned. It was the same dress I always wore, a short green dress with fake diamonds on the front. I felt sexy when I wore it and made good money. I thought it made my ass look great. Brandy disagreed out loud and often. That night, I decided not to get my makeup done, and like always my fingernails and toenails were not manicured or pedicured.

"What are you doing Mica, hoarding money?" Brandy said.

I looked in the mirror and got her point right away. "Fine," I said. "I'll get my makeup done."

I tipped the makeup artist $10 to do my makeup. I bought a new dress and panties from the house mom, which cost me $125. I felt brand new in my new purple dress with fake diamonds and matching purple panties.

"Good start," Brandy said. "Now go brush your hair."

I rolled my eyes and asked the makeup artist to curl my hair. So much for almost virgin hair. I wouldn't even try to explain this concept to her. I opened my mouth to protest and just stopped. I gave him another $10. Brandy was always reprimanding me to invest more in myself.

"Bitch, if you do well tonight you owe me ten percent," she said.

She owned too many dresses and panties to even fit them in one locker. Our club gave her two big lockers. She spent a lot on her appearance, like an honor-roll stripper. She was always well manicured and pedicured, always used the makeup artist at our club, and always wore very expensive perfume. She also wore expensive jewelry.

She explained that she saved receipts for everything she bought that was work related and used them as write-offs for her tax returns. Her appearance was an investment in her career.

## More Good Advice

Presentation is important in dancing. It's like you are an actress and you have to look and move the part. Brandy would reprimand me if I danced too fast or tried to twerk. She told me to follow how the Russian girls dance, slowly and calculated.

She also encouraged me to be patient and not to get up from a conversation with a customer I found annoying, and to lose the miserable look on my face.

"Jesus, no one likes a pouter," she said to me one night. "Go back and sit with him and smile."

The helpful hints did not end there, either,

"Dress like a stripper, not like a fairy princess," she'd tell me, or "For God's sake, go back downstairs and brush your hair and put more lipstick on. Lips should remind a guy of pussy lips. Red or pink lipstick, and make them wet with gloss."

Presentation is all part of the job, and Brandy was an expert. She also knew so much about connecting with clients. Brandy had such a range of life and sexual experiences that she could choose to talk about. She was good at reading a guy and appealing to him. She could intrigue a customer with her wild stories of stripping in Vegas and Atlanta, Georgia, which is the stripper capital of the United States, or she could talk about her kids or her childhood as a military brat.

If none of that worked, and she still couldn't make a connection, she might grab another stripper to come talk to the client with her. This is where her being diplomatic with other dancers helped her out a lot. If a customer liked a girl-next- door type, then she might grab me to come over and try to get him to take us both to a room.

Brandy knew how to work just about every angle there was to make money.

### Jackie
My best friend at work was Jackie. She was from Thailand. Jackie was my moral compass. She reminded me to go get life, and not to focus too much on money. When she was not working, she was traveling.

Jackie also went through the painful, slow process of teaching me to do my makeup so I didn't have to pay a makeup artist every night. On slow nights at the club she gave me haircuts in the dressing room. I'm convinced they were better than any fancy hair salon in New York City. She was hard working, positive, and a good listener.

Jackie was also transgender. We were both misfits. We did not fit in to a group. We weren't part of the Hispanic girls or the Russian girls and we each did not have a partner we worked with each night.

When other dancers talked behind my back, Jackie told me what they said.

"Mica makes bitchy faces," or "Mica is only nice to girls that make money."

If a manager was giving me a hard time, usually about wanting me to work more, Jackie gave me advice to deal with him. She reminded me I shouldn't take anything personally.

"Everyone gets talked about behind their backs," she said, "and managers want all the girls to work more."

Jackie made me feel less alone, and that was something I deeply appreciated.

**The Core Group**
At the club I worked at in New York City, there was what I called a core group of Russians and Eastern Europeans—Alyona, Dina, Irina, and Kristina. I called them the core group because, unlike the other Russian and Eastern European girls who worked at our club, they all lived together and traveled to and from work as a group and always worked the same nights.

The qualities they possessed, such as being organized, keeping an eye out for beautiful things, staying wellread and worldly, being well groomed, working in a team, and maintaining social graces, translated flawlessly to dancing and hustling. I continually tried to emulate them.

Alyona, who was from Bulgaria, was like an actress

who never came out of character. When she was on the floor, she was constantly conscious of the femme fatale role she was playing. She really got into it, but I knew she was just acting. Customers could not tell. Every move was calculated. She even changed her voice. When she worked, her voice was much higher. When a customer came in and took a seat, Alyona would point her toe of the leg that was crossed and stretch out her leg. She would take a deep breath and straighten her posture, and stick her chest out all while brushing her fingers through her hair. Her posture was always perfect and her makeup was always fresh. She always looked flawless, with not a hair out of place, and her makeup was never smudged. When she danced on stage or did lap dances, she moved slowly and sensually.

Alyona was stunning, with porcelain skin and crystal blue eyes. She was so feminine, very soft looking, as if she needed to be protected. Her body type was a little curvy but a little muscular, too. Her thick brown hair always looked freshly brushed and bouncy and flowed down her shoulders. She wore clear heels that complemented her diamond panties and diamond party jewelry. Her dresses were always the best colors for her complexion and paired perfectly—red with red lipstick, and blue dresses that matched her eyes.

She constantly played games. If a guy was wearing glasses, she would take them and act like a librarian. She would take her customer's suit jacket and wear it up on stage, and into private rooms, as it was her way of claiming the guy. She had a charming but silly seduction. Almost everything she said was flirtatious. It kept her laughing at herself, too, which kept her smiling, and smiling is sexy.

She would innocently wave at the guy who admired her most and sometimes played peek-a-boo with him or flirted with him so everyone could see. Oftentimes, her customer would be sitting next to the stage while she danced and wore his suit jacket or tie.

The rest of her friends—the core group—were in on Alyona's silly way of seducing. When they worked together to get a customer to a room, they all were like a band of actresses working together. Alyona and Irina were like a comedy duo when they did lap dances together. Alyona would find a group of Asian tourists (Asians love Eastern European girls) and she would scream to Irina.

"Irina, look how *cuuuuute*!"

"Oh my God," Irina would say, "They can be our boyfriends!"

"*Ahhhhh!*" they'd scream. "Let's go for double trouble on the couch!"

One song quickly turned into about five and within minutes they each made $100. Their playfulness made it look so easy.

When they gave lap dances, Alyona and Irina sometimes went an entire song without actually sitting on a guy's lap or taking off their dresses. They were smart enough to know that they would still make their 20 bucks or more because the guy liked them too much to notice that he was being fooled. After a lap dance, they always asked for tips on top of the $20 for each song.

Another strong point of Alyona's was that she had a lot of patience, which helped her get private rooms. Sometimes, she would sit with customers for more than an hour, listening intently. I often saw her with her hand on her chin of her flawless, porcelain face, staring back into a customer's eyes while listening. She would give a simple touch on the leg every once in a while, just to keep him going. Whenever I sat with her, I noticed that as soon as a negative subject came up, she changed it to something positive.

"Let's not talk about that," she'd say, when I mentioned rent in New York being so high. She'd quickly change the subject. When she joked and flirted, guys opened up to her, smiled more, and had more fun—and that meant more money.

She said anything that came to mind.

"Look how long your legs are, like a mermaid," or "I love your smile, it's like a bag of Christmas trees all lit up."

I loved talking to the core group. They were all very into self-improvement. Veronica loved motivational talks and literature about self-improvement. Dina, who used to be a bodybuilder, gave me diet advice. Kristina inspired me not to give up on my dream of learning French. Irina helped me plan my trip to Martinique. Alyona gave me very poignant, practical advice, especially on moving abroad.

Outside of that core group, there was Inga from Moscow, who traveled what seemed like everywhere. She would work about six to 10 days in a row, and then would go somewhere for a week or a month at a time. She would come back to work tan, happy, and looking so refreshed, compared to the girls who worked a lot. Her favorite places to travel were in South America. She spoke five languages—Russian, English, Spanish, Portuguese, and French. Impressive.

Inga helped me start living for my dreams. When we took the subway home together, she told me how she was once like me and worked a lot. Then she just started going places, like to the pyramids in Egypt, Machu Picchu, and Thailand, and to the beaches of South America.

**More Advice from the Core Group**

When it came to beauty and diet and saving money, I learned a lot from most of the Russian and Eastern European girls. They managed to spend less money and look amazing. The core group always brought their own makeup, and were really good at using it. They were also good at finding inexpensive, quality makeup.

I noticed that Kristina took her pharmacy brand, white eye shadow, which probably cost her less than $10 and doubled it as illuminating powder. Dry shampoo? They used baby powder. They were not the friendliest girls at the club, but they came with their clothes pressed, their hair done, and they were ready to make money, and that's it.

Irina tipped me off about getting manicures and pedicures.

"Why should I go for a manicure or pedicure if the paint is just going to chip after a day or two?" I said.

"When you go for a manicure or a pedicure, bring your own nail polish," she said. "This way, when your nails start to chip, you can fix it yourself at home. Also, bring your own tools because the salon's could be dirty."

Non-metal tools should be sterilized at home, things like foot files, nail files, and nail buffers. Make sure the metal tools at the salon are sanitized. Don't let them turn on the water jets, as this is where bacteria grows.

The core group of Russian and Eastern European girls sparkled. They wore fake diamonds and it made them look expensive. Even their panties had rhinestones on them. When strippers take their dresses off, we are still wearing an outfit—albeit a much smaller one. It's important to take as much time picking your panties, heels, jewelry, makeup, and hair as when you pick out a dress to wear. Pay attention to these things so that you look presentable even after you take your dress off.

The core group's dresses were very elegant. They looked like they were going to the Oscars. They took the time to see what dress went with their body types and their skin tones. The club's house mom sold dresses but the core group got theirs somewhere outside of the club and probably for a cheaper price.

Fake eyelashes are awesome. I actually learned this on my own but a lot of the R and EEG girls wore them. You can get them individually or in a small pack at a pharmacy for about 10 to 20 dollars. They are reusable a couple of times.

I would highly recommend you go on Amazon and get a box of 100 plastic ones for less than five dollars. They will come in sheets of pairs of lashes that will last you many months. Wear them only when you work at the club, as anyone can tell they are plastic. Clubs I worked at were dark and forgiving and I got away with wearing fake, poor-quality lashes there. You will struggle with putting them on at first. Watch a YouTube video and do it a couple times with another dancer or the makeup artist while you get ready in the changing room. You will need tweezers and eyelash glue. Fake eyelashes give a very dramatic effect.

## More Valuable Tips

One time, I remember it was four a.m. and a group of us were getting changed downstairs in front of our lockers, ready to go home, when Dina, one of the Russian girls, casually mentioned something about going to the gym as soon as she left.

A Bulgarian girl said, "I wouldn't be able to do that, I have to eat something after I work out and you should not eat and then go to sleep."

"But I always eat when I get home from work and before I go to bed," I said, "because I don't eat at work."

She looked at me like a mom looks at her kid and explained that this habit was not healthy and how it was affecting me. At the time, my skin was dry and I had stubborn stomach fat.

"You have to stop eating before you go to bed," she

said. "Eat at work around midnight or one o'clock and if you're hungry, eat a little around four a.m. when you get home from work. Then you could drink some water or non-caffeinated tea or have just a *small* spoonful of cottage cheese if you're still hungry."

I started to calculate what she was suggesting.

"Cottage cheese is easy for the body to digest," she said, "but just a tablespoon! It's fattening! While you sleep, your body works on what it cannot give energy to during the day. During the day, you use your energy to walk, work, read, and run. Whatever. You need the energy that you are not using while you are resting to take care of your organs and skin. By eating before bed, you make the body do work. It's digesting while you sleep. Then the body isn't taking care of the skin and organs."

I stared at her, as I had never heard this explained so simply.

"Understand?" she said.

I nodded. I was so motivated to change for aesthetic reasons that I started my new habits that night. Within a month of eating at midnight instead of at four a.m., right before I went to bed, my skin was radiating and my stomach was flat and muscular. Most important, I was healthier and sleeping better, too.

My colleague's tip had set me on a health quest to change my bad habits and improve my mind and body. I gave up coffee and substituted tea to clear up my skin even more. When I woke up each day, I worked out on an empty stomach. This jump-started my metabolism for the day.

I eventually started doing meal planning. I would've been lost without it. Dina, the Russian dancer who used to be a bodybuilder, sat with me one night when the club was slow and explained the basics of meal planning, which I will explain in Chapter 8.

You can always find good people in your club who will help you make progress, both physically and psychologically. There are always girls who will bond with you over healthy habits and other stuff, too. A common misconception is that Russian and Eastern European girls are mean because they care only about themselves. I actually got along well with them, even though they cared about themselves first. We all should keep ourselves number one, but we can also learn a lot from each other.

CHAPTER SIX: **Mastering the Hustle**

*"Ni\*\*a ask about me, Ni\*\*a ask about me,
I'm a hustla, I'm a, I'm a hustla homie."*
    —Jay-Z and Cassidy, "I'm a Hustler"

Master your hustle, whatever it may be, not just on the job, but outside of work, too.

I love to read. When I moved to New York, I invested in a Kindle and subscribed to the digital version of *The New York Times*. The news can serve as a conversation starter, even with guys you have nothing in common with or any interest in getting to know. It can also make you stand out because you have something worldly to talk about. I worked in Times Square, where tourists from Europe, Africa, and Asia joined a motley crew of local New Yorkers and guys traveling on business. World news came in handy and kept things interesting for me, too.

I got to apply what I learned. I hated when guys tried to get personal with me. I was supposed to be a fantasy and they did not deserve to know about my real life. Being well read strengthened my game and protected me from having to talk about myself.

*You never want to share details about your life.*

Don't tell people your real name, the town you were born in, the schools you went to, and certainly not where you live. Invent a story and stick to it because it's easier to work with your own invention. For example, say you meet a guy from your hometown and you tell him where you are from. You would most likely lose a lot of time chatting nostalgically with this guy about your town. Also, it might freak the guy out.

Instead, invent a benign, small town. In my experience, if a guy is being pushy about getting to know you too personally then you don't want to spend too much time trying to get a dance or a private room with him. Those types of guys usually don't spend money and may not really understand what the strip club experience is about. The more you get into the role of the character you are playing at the club, the more focused you can stay on your work, and when you're at a club, you are not lying—you are *acting*.

If it's a busy night, it's important not to spend too much time talking with any one customer. Give it two songs and then ask if he wants to do a dance. Of course there are exceptions, but generally give it just a couple of songs. Over time, you will know how to spot spenders.

If you have a choice of when to get ready to go home—either at last call for alcohol, which is about half an hour before the club closes, or when the club starts to tell people to leave—choose to leave when the club tells you. Drunk guys stay to the very end. You can easily make an extra 100 to 200 dollars or even get a private room in the last couple minutes. Our club stayed open if a guy wanted to do a room in the last minute. Cash out when you get a chance!

## Know Your Customers

It helps to know why guys come to the club. Some are there because they have some sort of sexual fetish. Our makeup artist told me there was a customer who came because he wanted to be breast-fed and pretend the dancer was his mother. Some guys come simply because they are men, and biologically, men want more than one sex partner. They want to be surrounded by all types of girls. Groups of guys come for bachelor parties. Some guys want to find a real connection with a woman and they like the openness that strippers offer. Some are looking for a girlfriend. Others want to escape their work and family lives, to forget their everyday existence. Some guys like to escape through alcohol and coke, so they are looking to you for a drink and drug buddy.

Some men don't know how to talk to women. Or they prefer to talk down to women and they are frustrated that they can't get away with this behavior on the street. I was often "put down" by men at work. Actually, I came to realize it was a sad reflection of their own frustrations in life.

When a guy asked me during my first month of stripping if I was pregnant, I became frustrated and confused. I definitely did not look pregnant. I was used to getting compliments on how fit I was. I quickly opened up to another dancer at my club about what this customer said to me. She was a veteran stripper, originally from Philly, where she had started dancing at a young age, and was 33 when we were working together in New Jersey at Layla's. I looked at her, seriously hurt, and told her what he said. She looked back at me and started laughing.

"Baby girl, who said that?"

I pointed, practically in tears.

"Ha! Look at him," she laughed. "Look at you. He can't get you outside of here so he wants to say mean shit to you. Guys do that shit all the time to us. You go to the gym like every day. You know your body is on point."

I nodded.

"When someone feeds you bullshit," she said, "you feed it right back. Say yeah, I actually have five kids and five baby daddies."

I smiled from ear to ear, knowing she was right.

## Women Are Customers, Too

Although I've usually seen women show up at a club with their boyfriend or husband, sometimes they come alone. I identify women customers who frequented the clubs I worked at into four categories:

1. The girlfriend or wife who wants to be cool and "open to new experiences."
2. The "closet lesbian."
3. The "angry, unhappy girlfriend or wife" taking it all out on the strippers.
4. The "really cool, awesome woman" who most likely used to be a stripper.

Women usually come to a club with their boyfriend or their husband. As a dancer, it sucks to try to sell dances or rooms to a couple. Selling to two people is more complicated than selling to one.

When you first approach a couple, always sit next to the woman. This makes you less threatening. Remember that you are wearing less clothing then she is; you look hot, and you are in front of her man. She has to feel comfortable. Nine times out of ten, she is the one making the final decision on buying dances or private rooms so she should always be your first priority. Talk to her like she is your friend and try to make a sincere connection. Once you get into a conversation with her, then the guy can relax, too!

For example, start a friendly conversation using one of the following:

"I love your bag, where did you get it?"

"Where are you guys from? How do you like New York City? What have you done since you got here?"

Then you can dig a little deeper if the conversation is going well:

"Have you ever danced before?"

"You look like you would be a good dancer! Have you ever wanted to try it? It's so fun!"

Don't start asking about their relationship until the woman brings it up. When you first sit down, do *not* say, "Your husband/boyfriend is so hot, I can't wait to dance for him!"

Be aware of the types of women you will encounter. I often came across the girlfriend who wanted to prove to her boyfriend or husband how "cool" she was. What better way than going to a strip club and kicking back some beers just like she is one of his guy friends? A lot of times, the man's face tells it all: he wishes he were there alone. They sneak longing looks at the strippers when they are sure their girlfriend/wife's attention is diverted. The woman, who is trying to be cool for her man, is usually not comfortable but she is trying to be. She will be a lot of work, usually intoxicated, and will touch you inappropriately to prove how "open" she is.

She may say something like, "I'm okay with disrespecting women and not following club rules." She may go a step further—after one too many drinks —and ask you to give her husband sexual favors. Beware of these women and keep them under control. Keep enforcing the *no touching* rule in a playful way.

"No, no, I can touch you, but you can't touch me, ha!"

Be firm, or else you will have a couple trying to get out of control with you.

You may run into an angry wife or girlfriend who is secretly jealous of the dancers. When you talk to her, she will be condescending and bitter and most likely intoxicated. It will sound like this:

> **Me:** Hi, how are you?
>
> **Her:** Hi, great, so what do you do?
>
> **Me:** Dances, rooms, whatever you like.
>
> **Her:** No, I mean outside of here; what do you do? Do you work? Do you go to school? Did you finish college?
>
> **Me:** Oh, yeah, I did.
>
> **Her:** Why the hell are you here? Why don't you go get a job?
>
> **Me:** I love dancing. I can show you how good I am if you come with me on the couch for a dance.
>
> **Her:** No, definitely not.

These women, usually dressed in expensive clothing, and proud of their own or their man's powerful career, get off on trying to assume a "high-class status." Just smile, nod, ask if they want a dance and move on.

Every once in a while, I experienced a closet lesbian, a type I eventually came to instantly recognize. These women usually came to the club alone and nervously talked to dancers, one after the other. They usually pounded drinks to get comfortable, enough to build up to being comfortable with a dance or private room. In my experience, these women spent a lot of money. Be gentle with them, as they are sincerely looking for a deep connection and finding their identities, and can become extremely physical after getting intoxicated.

Generally speaking, bouncers are less willing to restrain women if they get out of line during dances on the floor. If it's two girls, and one is half-naked and the other one is groping her, most straight male bouncers won't try to stop it. Women customers can sometimes be more aggressive then men and can get away with more. I once was picked up off of my feet by a woman and laid down on the couch, where she started dancing on top of me and stripping. It was like I was the exhausted matador and she was the wild, unpredictable bull. This never would have happened if it had been a male customer.

One of my favorite kinds of female customer is very in tune with her sexuality and respects the boundaries of our job. A lot of times, these women were strippers at one point in their lives. They are out for a nice time. I connected easily with these women. They are pleasant to talk to and it is easy to give them dances that are not aggressive, but sensual. They are almost always happy if you give dances to their boyfriend or husband, then they make sure you get tipped well.

The funniest advice I ever received came from a woman who once was a stripper. While I danced for her and her husband watched, she dispatched, "Always work on your resume and keep it up to date, and 'rich niggas love golf,' so know a little bit about it."

She was right.

### Creating "Silent Leverage"

By working at more than one club, I was no longer at the mercy of one owner or management team. I had "silent leverage." If they wanted me to work four days one week when I could only give them three, I could say no and still find work.

Reaching this point gave me confidence. I didn't get shook anymore by bossy managers.

*If you want me, you can give me what I want.*

I never said that explicitly, but they got the message—from a Jersey Girl at her finest.

When I worked at Velvet in New York City, I invested too much time and energy there. For more than two years, I usually worked four times a week. The managers took my blind dedication for granted and demanded more and more of my time, to a point where they were bullying me when I didn't make a schedule that fit their needs.

But I kept dancing there because I was accustomed to it and some of the girls had become close friends. Even when business was slow, I kept going back.

Finally, I built up enough courage to leave for another club nearby, called Hush. It was such a good decision. The girls and the managers were much more professional. I didn't see any sloppy dancers; the managers never touched me, and I had to fill out a W-2, so legit taxes were taken out of my pay.

For the first time in my dancing career, I would be on the books!

There would be no more paying estimated quarterly taxes, unless I worked off the books at another place. This was a huge relief. From what I saw in the first month working there, Hush tried to take care of the girls that worked for them. They provided snacks in the changing room, and the house mom, DJ's, bouncers, and hosts were friendly. At Velvet, the bouncers seated customers next to girls that tipped them, but at Hush, this was not the case. The customers could still be sleaze balls, but that I could handle.

I liked the change of scenery, and being a novelty to the regular customers was cool. Guys were so excited to see a new girl, and since I was comfortable there, my personality came through much more. I was friendlier and more excited to talk to customers. I probably had the bubbliest personality among the dancers.

I dressed in a more sophisticated and sparkly manner, like my Russian friends. I felt confident enough to reinvent my style. I even changed my name from Mica to Kelsey.

Since I felt better about myself and was no longer carrying the heavy weight of issues with management, or suffering from drama with the dancers, I could just concentrate on connecting with the most important part of the whole show—the customers. I could listen intently, make genuine eye contact, and move with purpose. I asked customers to tell me more about their lives, and every gesture was made with intent.

I winked, waved, moved my hips, and blew kisses as I moved through the club, "bumping" into a guy at just the right time, or "bending over" to pick up a "dropped dollar" in front of a customer every girl wanted to shake hands with, but couldn't reach. My creative juices were flowing, and I had a new sense of calm.

Just three blocks away from Velvet, it felt like a different world, which was all due to finally figuring out that I had the power—as much or more—than any freaking manager.

### Vacationing

Dancing is tough work, and you need a vacation like anyone else.

Once I went for a week to Montreal, Canada, where I planned on practicing my French while exploring the city. It was surprisingly expensive there, so I decided to see if a local club would hire me for a few days so I could pay for my trip and still have plenty of time to—vacation! I danced at La Maison, one of the best high-end clubs in the city.

Back in New York, a few dancers tipped me off about trying out Myrtle Beach, South Carolina during peak golf season. One girl I worked with returned a week later with ten grand, which she had earned in just five nights! Another girl I know vacationed in Hawaii for two weeks and easily paid for her trip with a few nights of dancing at a local club.

When it comes to taking a working vacation, this is the way to go!

## The Golden Rule
*Do not ever see a guy outside of the club.*

You will be asked many times by customers to go on vacations or sleep with them at a hotel room and be paid. Just don't even think about it. It's dangerous. You don't know these men.

Don't give them your phone number, either. If you want to contact them to get them back into the club, I suggest you create an email account just for your clients. If they really want to see you again and you will not go outside the club, then they will come there to see you and spend money there. Remember: you are the boss, and you have complete control of the situation.

Don't drink or do coke with them, either. If they are drinking and it's been a slow night, you can fake a shot of tequila. Order a bottle of water and a shot of tequila. Drink half of your water. Than get the tequila shot in your mouth and when you "chase with water" you are really just spitting tequila back into the water bottle.

I don't recommend going to a room with cocaine. But you can fake doing cocaine. With a rolled-up dollar bill, put your back toward the guy and blow out, blowing the coke off the table. Practice at home with sugar. If you do decide to do this in a room, be careful the guy doesn't see. Best not to ever go into a room with a guy who will be doing coke.

You are a fantasy for these guys.

If they come there and have a fetish—beware. You can still try to get them into a private room and not perform their freaky fetish. Try to connect with them on some deeper level. Figure out what they are passionate about and talk about it. Be lighthearted, and don't talk about reality too much.

For example, a customer sits down with you and a conversation starts.

> **Customer:** So how's your night going?
> **You:** It's good most nights but today I've only made two hundred dollars. That sucks because I have to pay a $140 house fee just to work here and then I have to pay for parking. So I really just broke even. I have to wake up early tomorrow, too, 'cause I have a doctor's appointment.
> **Customer:** "Oh, wow, I'm so sorry."

That is not what you want to say. It is too real and makes the customer uncomfortable. If you are talking, you should be positive. Instead it should go like this:

> **Customer:** So how's your night going?
> **You:** It's been a good night, so far, and it's not over, yet! It's been a party here tonight and I'm happy all my friends are working with me tonight. How is your night going?

This is a much better way to talk to a customer. He can see that you are in the mood to have fun, and that you are wondering about him. The cash will flow much better this way.

## How to Manage Private Rooms
Before I even get into describing what goes on in private rooms, I have to lay down the law for any dancer in this profession:

Get your tip *before* you enter a private room.

When it comes to making money, I found the most ideal situation in New York City clubs to be the private rooms, where a full hour costs the customer $1,100, with $600 going to the house and $500 for me, which is a pretty nice takeaway, especially considering how often I received another $500 as a tip, which the guy was happy to pay—*before* I even set foot in the room.

I had a lot of customers like this, men who happily took care of me with cash in advance, which is usually a telltale sign that they will be pretty laid back once you get rolling in the private room.

The same type of scene occurred quite often with this type of good customer. For example, when I would go inside the room and start removing my dress, this kind of classier guy would say something like, "You don't have to dance or take your dress off. I just want you to be comfortable. I'm comfortable if you're comfortable." Or when the host would drop off drinks in the private room, the man would respond in a similar fashion, with a comment like "You don't have to drink if you don't want to." That was a nice relief, as it spared me the usual trick of pretending to drink by swishing the alcohol in my mouth and then spitting it out when the guy wasn't looking.

I've described the easy times in the private rooms, when an hour passes by like nothing, and taking money from these guys is like swiping candy from a baby.

But private rooms could also be a nightmare. That's why it's vital that you always get your tip *before* you enter. That way, if for some reason you are not doing what a guy wants or expects you to do in a private room, and he cancels in the first five or ten minutes, gets all his money back, and picks a different girl, you are not left with nothing. Once you get the tip, you will probably be able to keep it, even if he changes his fickle mind and chooses someone else. That should become his problem, not yours.

The proudest moment of my stripping career took place when a guy cancelled our private room after ten minutes with me. Before I went into the room that night with him, I had to prove that I was the "right" one, that among all the girls he could choose, I was the one he wanted most. It was as if he were conducting a job interview on the lap dance couches. Girls came over to him and he bought them drinks. Eventually, he narrowed his selection down to me and two other dancers. We were all sitting with him on a couch and knew he would take one of us, meaning a nice chunk of cash was on the line. We just didn't know which one of us would get it.

At the same time he went to the bathroom, one of the girls had to go dance onstage, leaving me with a beautiful Russian girl.

"He is nasty," she said. "He doesn't want to take me to the room. He took me already and he didn't like me because I wouldn't do things with him. Maybe he will not come back to the couch at all."

I thanked her, but figured I needed to find out for myself. I followed him toward the bathroom and found him at the bar in another section of the club. He had already downed quite a few drinks and it was only nine p.m. I wasn't worried about getting into a private room with him. I just wanted to float the idea and see if I could get a big tip.

"Hey there," I said. "Where did you go? I missed you."

"Honestly," he said, "you are my first choice. You are the one I want in the private room. You are the most beautiful one."

I smiled, thinking I had him.

"But I have to warn you," he said. "I am nasty, and I don't know if you'll like it."

"Oh please," I said. "I wanna have fun. Let's go have a really good time."

"Are you sure?" he said.

"Of course I am. It's what I want. I want to have fun."

We went back and forth like this for about five more minutes, until I waved the host over to get things moving. He paid her $1,700 for one hour in a private room with me.

"Before we go," I said, not missing a beat, "just so we don't have to worry about money later, let's just be all finished with it now, okay? So can you just tip me three or four hundred dollars?"

"I can't believe it," he said, downing another drink. "Yeah, sure I will. I'll tip you three hundred now and then later, too. I want a lot in the room."

Within five minutes being alone with him in the private room, I had everything under control.

"Keep your pants on," I told him. "Let's move slow. I want to have fun, but it's much sexier to go slow."

He grew tired of my act pretty fast and switched me for a different girl. I walked away with $300 dollars in less than ten minutes. My manager also gave me $100 for my time spent in the room.

Once again, always ask for your tip *before* you enter a private room.

### Dancing Onstage Is Fun and Easy

While dancing on stage you need to read the room, no matter how much fun the dancing may be. Watch how the girls who have worked at your club for at least one year are dancing on stage. Are they doing floor work? Pole tricks? Twerking? Just moving slowly with the music?

In the beginning, copy from them what you know you can do.

I don't want to sound like your mother, but don't

try right away to be a superstar on stage. Just be comfortable while conforming with what you see going on.

If you work at a club where pole tricks are commonplace, go on Groupon and invest in some pole dancing lessons. Pole dancing will get you into amazing shape outside of the club and it will help market you onstage. But do tricks only once you've mastered them. Could you imagine being on stage and doing an inversion and then being afraid to come out of it for fear of falling? You could get seriously hurt if you don't know what you're doing.

It took me over a year to evolve as a dancer, to the point where I finally looked sexy and confident onstage. All I did was copy other dancers' moves that I liked and knew I could do, and I moved slowly. I did not know many dance moves when I started, so when I moved slowly I looked like a better dancer. It was definitely an illusion, but I worked it to my advantage.

When I started dancing, I was really into going to the gym and running. As a result, when I danced, I was stiff on stage, and it showed. Also, I could not—and still cannot—twerk. I tried and tried. I watched YouTube videos. I secretly studied girls while they danced on stage. I practiced in front of a mirror. I just could not arch my back enough to do it. At first, I thought my butt didn't have enough fat on it to twerk. But I've seen thin girls who can twerk just as well as curvy girls and white girls who can twerk just as well as black girls. All you need is some fat on your butt, not a lot, and the ability to arch your back. I could not do it but I encourage you to try it. It might be your hidden talent.

You could always go on Amazon and buy a portable stripper pole. I bought a professional dance-stripping pole and had it installed in my studio apartment. It cost only $144, not including the installation. I practiced at home—more for fun than for work. I learned tricks that I wouldn't have been able to teach myself at work.

## Tipping

Tipping people can be frustrating. After all, you were the one who spent time in a room with a guy. You were the one who took your clothes off. You paid a house fee and are an independently contracted worker. The club does not cover your medical insurance like a regular job would. You acquire expenses from working at a club: transportation, makeup, and clothes. When you do a room, you get only about half the money. Why should you give away more of your hard-earned money to your manager or your host?

In my experience, you should tip what is required and that is it. I used to tip my manager once a week, and I didn't have to. I tipped him when he cashed me out, when he changed my stripper money (funny money) into real money. Funny money is credit card money that can be used on the floor for dancing or tipping dancers for private rooms. At the end of the night, dancers change their funny money for cash. That's what we call "cashing out."

After a couple weeks, my manager made it awkward if I got cashed out without tipping him. After he handed me my cash, there would be an intentional awkward silence. One time, he even sarcastically said, "You're welcome" when he gave me my cash and I did not tip him. I had to undo him associating me with tipping him. I stopped giving him tips. I wished I had never started.

In those times, I always think of some lyrics from the Notorious B.I.G., Diddy, Mase, in *"Mo' Money, Mo' Problems"*: "I don't know what they want from me. It's like the more money we come across, the more problems we see."

Tipping the manager is meant for girls who do sexual favors or drugs in the private rooms. Managers have video cameras. They can see what goes on. If a girl is doing more than dancing, she will tip the manager.

Each club is different. Even if two clubs have the same basic rules about lap dances and private rooms, no two clubs are the same because they have different people working there. Get to know the rules and the people working there. It will make your life much easier.

CHAPTER SEVEN: **Get Your Money Straight**

*"No need to worry,*
*my accountant handles that."*
　　—Biggie Smalls, "Juicy"

Get your money goals straight.

At this point, you've had the chance to enjoy a couple of months of doing responsible things and splurging a bit with your profits—buying heels, dresses, makeup for work, moving expenses, and transportation. Now it's time to form a bigger plan for your money.

At first, I bought a giant safe, thinking I would put all of my money in it. But keeping your money at home in a safe is unsafe and illegal and you should not do it. Money stayed in my safe from the time I got home from work till the time I put it in a bank. I love to run, and every day I ran to the bank to deposit money. The bank was part of my running route. In 2015 and 2016, I invested most of my money in a 401K and a SEP Account. I'll tell you more about this in a bit.

First, I can't stress enough that you should get an accountant so you can sleep peacefully at night knowing that if the IRS decides to audit you, you have someone who can defend your income and expenses.

*You have to pay taxes or the IRS will come after you.*

*To avoid that very bad situation, file your tax returns and pay your taxes.*

*I repeat: you have to pay your taxes or the IRS will come after you.*

The IRS will not immediately contact you for not filing one or even two years of tax returns. But many years down the line, it could be five years or it could be ten years later, the IRS will contact you and ask you to explain why you did not file tax returns or pay taxes for these years that you were earning cash. This is not a situation you want to be involved in and this is the situation that a good accountant can help you avoid.

I suggest you get an accountant who will help teach you how to organize your income and expenses. To find an accountant, get on Yelp and see who has the best reviews in your area. Ask him or her how long they have been practicing, and if they can represent you if the IRS comes after you. Ideally, they should have at least five years under their belt. Also, try to find an accountant who has experience dealing with cash businesses. The cash nature of your dancing job has a lot of unique issues that only an accountant who has experience dealing with cash businesses, like restaurants, laundromats, and strip clubs, will understand.

*There is nothing illegal about having a job that pays in cash, just some unique challenges, like how to store, report, and pay taxes on that income.*

My accountant met with me for a free consultation. I

told him that I was a dancer and that I was petrified of the IRS. In 2015, I did not pay my taxes and I was really nervous about being penalized. If you missed paying taxes for the first year you started dancing, let my experience be your wake-up call. I was assured that I could pay in a lump sum in April for 2015 and there was not a very big penalty. Then he taught me how to organize my income and expenses in an Excel spreadsheet for tax organization purposes. Any type of bookkeeping system, whether it is a simple spreadsheet, an app like XERO, or pencil and paper is a good bookkeeping system as long as it keeps track of how much and when you earn income and spend money on expenses.

*You have to be disciplined in order to maintain the bookkeeping system accurately.*

Spend a little bit of time doing bookkeeping every week so that your records are always up to date and accurate. My accountant helped me to become autonomous in paying my taxes each quarter so that I could do everything on my own and check in with him at the end of the year in his office. It is not hard to manage your taxes on your own with a little guidance every once in a while from a professional.

I tracked my income for 2015 all in one shot. To do this, I printed out my bank statement at the end of the year to record my monthly income. You'll see in July I had deposited more than $20,000. Yes, that is correct. Prior to that deposit, I had that money in my safe at home. That deposit was what made me realize I had no idea how to handle making cash as income and I needed an accountant. Walking to the bank on a sunny, summer day in New York City with a backpack full of cash is a weird situation to be in.

This chart is a sample of how I tracked my yearly income and expenses. I sent the final draft with the actual income numbers to my accountant to review.

That way, he could prepare my tax return efficiently. The IRS begins accepting tax returns toward the end of January, and tax laws vary from state to state, so pay close attention!

| INCOME | | EXPENSES |
|---|---|---|

| | AMOUNT | SOURCE | DEPOSIT |
|---|---|---|---|
| 1/24/15 | 3,246 | Dancing | Citibank |
| 2/24/15 | — | Dancing | Citibank |
| 3/24/15 | 15,493 | Dancing | Wells Fargo |
| 4/24/15 | 6,065 | Dancing | Wells Fargo |
| 5/24/15 | 1,059 | Dancing | Citibank |
| 6/24/15 | 1,200 | Dancing | Citibank |
| 7/24/15 | 21,480 | Dancing | Wells Fargo |
| 8/24/15 | 3,584 | Dancing | Wells Fargo |
| 9/24/15 | 3,270 | Dancing | Citibank |
| 10/24/15 | 640 | Dancing | Citibank |
| 11/24/15 | 1,762 | Dancing | Citibank |
| 12/24/15 | 3,120 | Dancing | Citibank |

I entered 2016 ready to track my income and expenses and to save my receipts for the whole year. I bought an accordion-style, expanding file folder and categorized each pocket. I put receipts in sections marked as the following:

✓ Dance lessons
✓ Kindle device and Kindle books
✓ House fees for the club
✓ Makeup artists
✓ Manicures and pedicures for work
✓ Transportation (subways, buses, and taxis), sometimes to other clubs
✓ Work clothes (shoes, dresses and jewelry)
✓ Health insurance (paid through state marketplace, whenever possible)
✓ Money sent to charities throughout the year
✓ Miscellaneous (massage, Botox, etc.)

Check with your accountant to make sure you're up to date on current tax laws, which change from year to year.

I also kept track of what I paid in quarterly estimated tax payments. As a self-employed dancer, you have to make tax payments to the government every three months. These are the same kind of tax payments that employed people make from their paychecks. Receipts and bank statements must correspond to income and expenses created on spreadsheets. My bookkeeping was accurate, which gave my accountant and me the confidence to defend all of my expenses as things I had to buy for work.

In the case of an audit, what matters is how you link these expenses to what is necessary to manage your business. You and your accountant can make the best argument for the expenses you've listed. Then it is up to the IRS to decide which ones they will accept. It's not likely that they will *all* be accepted, but that does not mean that you and your accountant cannot make a case for all of them, as you can cite your concrete evidence, the law, and current regulations. Some expenses, like manicures or pedicures, and taxis, may be harder to argue, but things like shoes and dresses, dance lessons, makeup artists, and house fees, will be easier.

According to Jerry Chin, E.A., owner of Astoria Tax in New York, you and your accountant always have the right to appeal an IRS determination, but since that takes place in court it's likely that your accountant will settle something for you before it reaches that level.

In any case, always keep accurate records!

### Financial Goals

My first big-picture financial goal with my stripper money was 100k in retirement, and then to save for France. I later took all of the money out of retirement to use it to start my life in France. If I had stayed in New York, I would have kept it all in retirement.

Interest compounds, so the earlier you put money away, the more you can let it start compounding interest. I knew that I wanted my money to work for me. Investing it would have been the smartest move to make—that is, before I decided to use the money toward my move.

Money for retirement is not taxable until you take it out at age 65. I used a time-sensitive mutual fund through the company Vanguard. I paid a fee for them to invest my money, but then I didn't have to do any work. The investments are riskier when you are young, and safer when you get older. When you are young and able to take more risks with your investment money, the mutual fund will invest in more high-risk/high-reward investments, like stocks in foreign countries and technology stocks. When you are older, you should take fewer risks with your money because you have fewer opportunities to make up for losses. At that time, the mutual fund will invest in safer investments, like bonds and dividend-bearing stocks. My older brother works in finance, and he tipped me off on where to invest my money.

## Long-term Goals

Your long-term goal might be to own an apartment, save for a business, pay off student loans, or pay off any credit card debt. To me, buying real estate seemed really complicated, as it takes time, about three years to prove that you make enough to get a loan from a bank. Then you may have that mortgage for 15 to 30 years. There is a process in order to own a house. But it could be a wise decision.

Financial gurus recommended the following:

1. Keep a liquid form of emergency fund.
2. Pay off debts, such as student loans and credit cards (for young people who don't yet have other expenses)
3. Start putting money away for retirement. (Get that compound interest working!)
4. Save for a house.

## No One Dances Forever

Remember: this job has a lifespan, and to be a smart stripper you should not waste the money you earn. I liked to say to myself that this money is not mine. For some reason, that helped me a lot with saving.

Like anything else in life, you need to have some fun. So treat yourself *once in a while* to a trip, clothes you really want, or a massage. But try to put almost all of your hard-earned money toward what will help you long-term.

## Looking to the Future

My original goal was that when it comes time to enter the real workforce in my early 30's, I would not have to worry about making any more huge contributions to my retirement fund or my emergency fund. I will just have to worry about living expenses in my life abroad.

With retirement and emergency fund out of the way I would not be so daunted in starting a new job where I would have to be very focused and calm to be successful.

CHAPTER EIGHT: **Do Your Body Right**

*"You got attitude on na na,*
*And your pu\*\*y on agua,*
*And your stomach on flat flat,*
*And your ass on what's that?*
*And, yeah, I need it all right now."*
    —DJ Khaled featuring Drake, "Another One"

I wish I had the discipline of my coworker, a Russian girl who used to be a bodybuilder. She taught me a lot about nutrition. When she was training for a bodybuilding show, she followed her coach's advice for portioning her food each day to give her body just what it needed to be perfectly nourished. For example, she didn't chew gum, as there is sugar in gum and that would have hidden her abs.

What I learned from her and my own experiences boils down to this: Your eating habits affect 90 percent of your body's health and working out is just the "icing on the cake." A person who exercises irregularly, such as walking to work or biking to the store, but eats clean and well-portioned meals all day, can have a fit, lean body and never need to go to a gym. Meanwhile, I've met gym rats who are chubby because they exercise a lot but don't eat right.

Good eating habits will produce radiant skin and an energetic, high-functioning body, allowing you to enjoy your life and to feel beautiful inside and out.

As a dancer—and as a person, in general—I had to work on my diet, because while my workout was together, my diet was not. Here, in a nutshell, is what I learned—from books, other dancers, and listening to my own body.

### Meal Planning

It works! I've evolved to eat five meals a day. When you eat less food more frequently, your metabolism speeds up. Figure out how much you should be eating five to six times a day by first figuring out your Base Metabolic Rate. This refers to how much your body burns when you are at rest. Your body burns calories simply from breathing, sleeping, circulating blood, and basic brain functions.

Then figure out your target calorie intake for your goal weight. Maybe you want to gain weight in muscle, or you might want to lose weight for more muscle definition, or you may simply choose to maintain your weight.

Next, determine your calorie intake for rest days, and what it will be on active days that you workout. For example, I eat 500 calories more on my active days. I eat between 1350 and 1500 calories on rest days, and 1500 to 2000 on active days. I also have a cheat day where I eat 2500 to 3000 calories.

For me, becoming comfortable with converting to the metric system (grams) and using an app on my phone to see the breakdown of foods has been very helpful. I concentrate on protein, fats, and carbs, which are called macronutrients— macros, for short.

"Hitting your macros" means monitoring your intake of these macronutrients to keep the proper balance in your body. According to www.forum.bodybuidling.com, when people post about cutting or bulking up (getting "huge!" LOL), someone usually asks about caloric intake (deficit or surplus) and macros to help determine if it's nutrition that is impeding the person's goal.

I need these in the right percentage each day to help my body function at an optimal level, but it is also vital to get these nutrients into my body at the right time of the day.

I cook all my dinners on Sunday for the week. Usually, I do chicken (baked), yams (baked), vegetables (steamed), and rice (boiled). I portion everything with my food scale and put the portioned meals into glass containers. When the food cools, I freeze three meals and keep three meals in the fridge. Altogether, I cook six dinners on Sunday for Monday to Saturday.

This was my grocery list of clean foods:

### Proteins
*(No cured meats or cold cuts because they contain a lot of salt)*

Chicken breasts
Salmon
Cod
Tuna steak
Turkey
Canned tuna
Shrimp

## Veggies
*(Whatever you like—you can't go wrong)*

Asparagus
Broccoli
Cauliflower
Spaghetti squash
Brussels sprouts
Yams

## Grains
*(No refined grains, as they are stripped of many nutrients. Whole grains haven't had their bran and germ removed.)*

Brown rice
Quinoa

## Healthy Fats
Avocado
Yogurt
Cottage cheese
Coconut oil (for cooking)

I recommend Bodybuilding.com as an awesome resource. It gives formulas to figure out your necessary caloric intake to achieve your weight goal or to maintain your current weight, or to gain muscle.

Also, don't forget: your food needs to be prepared and stored properly.

## Items for Cooking and Storing Food
Glass containers for freezer storage (no plastic!)
Rice cooker (doubles as a storage bowl)
Livestrong App (measures grams in food)
Food scale
Measuring cup

## Managing Weight

I'm 5'7", and I was about 145 pounds when I started dancing. I weighed myself once a week in the beginning to see if I was changing at all. But once I saw that I was losing weight, I stopped going on the scale. Weight is a tricky thing because muscle weighs more, so you could take your body fat percentage if you prefer to do that. I went by weight for the first couple of weeks.

I wanted to weigh 135. According to Dina, my bodybuilder friend, on a rest day when I'm not working out I should consume 1350 calories. That amount was to lose weight, and eventually, when I weighed 135, I would eat 1350 for maintenance. On the days I ate 1350, my resting metabolic rate was sustained, but that was all. Resting metabolism (BMR) is the total number of calories your body burns at rest.

I ate 1850 to 2000 calories on active days when I did HIIT (High Intensity Interval Training) or was running five to six miles.

Forty-five percent of my calories were from carbs, 30 percent were from proteins, 25 percent came from fat, and I broke this down into five meals.

On an active day, I ate about 40 grams of carbs per meal for five meals, 27 grams of protein per meal for five meals, and 10 grams of fat for five meals. I posted my plan on my refrigerator.

It was an estimated plan. You can come up with a plan on your own by using formulas you find from trusted resources, such as a friend or a former bodybuilder, or consult a professional, such as a dietitian. It's up to you how far you want to take your nutritional and fitness goals.

## My Daily Routine

While dancing full-time, I usually woke up and drank plain tea with no milk, honey, or sugar and then worked out on an empty stomach to rev up the metabolism. Then I ran for about a half-hour. I varied my runs. Sometimes, they were on a treadmill, sometimes outside, sometimes I did hills, and sometimes I did intervals. After I ran, I drank a small protein shake consisting of two scoops of protein powder, water, and a scoop of peanut butter. Then I lifted light weights at high repetition. There are many benefits to weightlifting: muscle tone, injury prevention, speedier metabolism, and strength—just to name a few.

Don't be intimidated by any of this. I love to work out and want muscle definition. If you just walk for half an hour every day, that is great, too. But don't be shy about pushing yourself.

After I worked out at the gym and had my protein shake, I usually went home and had my next meal, which was about three hours after that shake. I continued the day eating every four to five hours.

Of course I cheated on some days. I wasn't training for a bodybuilding competition. I just wanted to feel good and be healthier and look toned. But I didn't have to hit a certain weight. I just chose meal planning, weighing my food, and calculating my macros as my dietary guidelines. It helped me a lot.

I started bringing a small snack to work with me. I would take a break at the club to eat at about two a.m. It was healthier for me to take a break from working, too. That snack was the last thing I would eat for the night. I went home at four and fell asleep by five.

I don't want to sound like your mother but when you sleep on an empty stomach, your body can take care of itself much better. When we sleep, the metabolic rate is much slower. If you eat right before you go to bed, your body accumulates the additional nutrients and transforms them to body fat.

But! If I am so hungry that I cannot get to sleep, I

eat a spoonful of cottage cheese to fill my belly or drink some water. Thankfully, it's easy for the body to digest cottage cheese, as there is a lot of protein in it. But it's fattening, so only a spoonful! Or just drink some water to fill your stomach.

## Get Organized and Get Healthy!
Nutrition is more complicated than just eating meals, so you have to focus on it to get it right. Above all, nourish your body for health reasons and be nice to yourself while you learn what works for your body. I love seeing all of my dinners cooked and packed for the week. When I bring them to work with me, I'm happy I don't have to order food. I know that I am taking care of myself. I know the ingredients in my food. Also, my energy level is much better when I eat smaller meals throughout the day.

Once you start meal planning you get better and faster at it (like with anything). Also, it saves you time and money during the week. Meal planning also lets you avoid having a weak moment and wanting to eat some unhealthy, fattening snack. Instead, you will be prepared to say no and eat what is there: a healthy, prepared snack. Be sure to weigh your food with a food scale and measuring cups. There has to be precision in weighing your food for meal planning to work, and as you get better at it, you can begin to eyeball portions.

I highly recommend the book *Skinny Bitch*, which promotes a vegan diet, but it is a great resource to begin being conscious about what you eat. It's a valuable resource, even if you don't want to become a vegan.

## Sound of Mind and Body
Keep your interests alive while you are growing financially. Take classes, travel, write a book, keep your dreams alive,

go for something bigger, and remember that, unlike many other careers, stripping does not have a long lifespan.

Find a club that lets you pick your schedule each week. I worked at clubs that let me do that, even when the managers wanted me to do more. If I had French lessons on Mondays, then I would take off Monday night and work Tuesday to Saturday. Or, if I was going on vacation for a week, I would not come in that week at all. The point is, you can and should be working on other, bigger projects. I was calmer knowing that I was able to work and concentrate on my French studies. Taking time for your future is a matter of respecting yourself.

Like Big Daddy Kane says, "Brain cells are lit. Ideas start to hit/Next the formation of words that fit/At the table I sit, making it legit/And when my pen hits the paper. Ahh shit!"

*Your stripping life can't be everything!*

Especially if you live in a city, I would recommend finding a club that will be flexible about your weekly schedule. That way, it is easier to plan your life outside the club. Some will try to make you work a certain number of days a week. Try to work in a place where you can make a schedule each week and pick how many days you will work.

You will get used to the late-night schedule, but at first you will be exhausted. And it is hard to have a social life when you are working at night and on weekends. The club has the potential to become a sort of other dimension if you work too much. Just don't get addicted to it—this is almost guaranteed to lead to depression. Even if you are making a lot of money, it's okay to take a break and "get a life." It is all too easy to think *I know I've worked eight days straight, but if I miss tonight I could miss out on making a thousand dollars.*

Please try not to think like this, as it will trap you.

The girls who push themselves at our club to work almost every night and hardly take breaks or nights off do not leave time to develop a life outside of stripping. This only adds to the pressure of having to make more money. It is a vicious cycle.

*Life is multifaceted; it is not just about money.*

## Life Is About More Than You

Donating money to charity will make you feel good. Pick a cause and get on its website to set up a donation. Tell people at the club about your cause. If possible, take some time off work and volunteer in your community or a place you've never been.

You will come back to work with a renewed sense of nonmaterial appreciation. That shows. When I returned to work after hiking in Arizona, skiing in Wyoming, or scuba diving in Martinique, I stood out to customers because I was so happy and excited about things that truly mattered in life, like enjoying nature, being with great people, and experiencing the world. I didn't have that money-hungry, zombie look. I was fresh-faced and excited about life.

I didn't have to try too hard at work on those nights. I was happy and money came easily to me, and that's the way I like it!

CHAPTER NINE: **Dancing for My Dream**

*"The most beautiful thing*
*that I'd seen on this planet,*
*She laughed cause you could tell*
*that I didn't know how to dance yet".*
*—Macklemore and Ryan Lewis, "The End"*

I'm no expert, but I do have real experience working in strip clubs. I wanted to write down my thoughts and observations about it to help girls who want to use stripping to pursue their dreams but might be scared to start. I hope this book has answered enough of your important questions about working in this industry.

If I may have missed anything, you can email me at:

danceradvice7@gmail.com

As for my dream of living in the Rhône-Alpes, I am getting very close! I'm living in New York, obtaining my student visa to study French in France. With the help of my accountant, I've saved money, paid my taxes, and have the funds I will need to get started abroad. I recently finished my CELTA (Certification in English Language Teaching for Adults) and will continue freelance writing. I would like to teach English and continue as an independent professional in writing.

And no matter what, I am determined to surround myself with positive people. I recommend you do the same. Be confident. Remember the best lessons come from the toughest situations; and dance your way closer to your dreams.

When I look back now to when I started all of this, I see how far I've come, more as a person than as a dancer, and how equipped I am for the adventure ahead of me. Ups, downs, times of confusion, and moments of clarity—I embraced all of it. I couldn't imagine my life without these experiences.

One last thought: Don't be afraid to try stripping. It's given me the opportunity to pursue my dream. I hope you can do the same.

# GLOSSARY

**Baller:** A guy who spends a lot of money.

**Band:** $1,000.

**Benjamin:** $100.

**Empty Suit:** A guy who looks like he has money because he is dressed well. If a bouncer does not like a dancer, he will sit an empty suit next to her as a distraction from a real baller.

**Floor Work:** A category of dance movements in which more than just your feet are in contact with the floor. It is performed on stage and often gives dancers a rest from performing tricks and dancing on the pole.

**Funny Money:** Money customers buy with their credit cards. It looks like Monopoly money, and the club charges an interest fee for it. Customers can buy dances with funny money; and dancers exchange funny money for cash when they cash out with their manager at the end of the night.

**Groupon:** An app full of coupons, which you can use to find inexpensive pole-dancing lessons.

**Host:** The person in charge of the private rooms, the one you take your customer to when you want to do a private room.

**House Fee:** What you pay to the house each night to work there.

**House Mom:** Takes care of the strippers throughout the night. Stays in the dressing room and deals with everything from a ripped dress to fetching a band-aid for a foot blister (or whatever) to handling melodramatic breakdowns from dancers.

**Long-Dress Night:** Designated night for wearing only long dresses.

**Mutual Fund:** Professionally managed investments in a basket of financial goods.

**Pleaser:** Popular stripper shoe company; can be ordered from on Amazon.

**Private Room:** Location for a more expensive, private lap dance. Also known as a champagne room.

**Rotation:** When the DJ puts girls on stage.

**Semi-Private Room:** Shared private room with dividers.

**SEP:** A retirement plan for employers and self-employed individuals.

**Set:** How long you have to dance on stage.

**Short-Dress Night:** Designated night for wearing only short dresses.

**Strapped:** Ebonics word for getting ready for work—i.e., getting dressed, packing your bag, etc.

**Ticket:** One million dollars.

**Vanguard:** Mutual fund company.

## ACKNOWLEDGMENTS

There are so many people to whom I owe my heartfelt thanks for helping me chase my dream. But a few deserve special mention.

René, en Français on dit: Qui va loin ménage sa monture. Maintenant organise toi pour réussir et pour aller aussi loin que possible.

Mike: thanks to you, I think big.

Lil' Tiff: My best friend, in and out of the club.

And to everyone I *don't* want to thank: thank you for challenging me…

## ABOUT THE AUTHOR

**Kerri Walker** has been dancing professionally for three years. She began in New Jersey, and after saving up for six months, she moved to New York City to live and dance there. It took her a year to save $100,000 in order to fulfill her long-held dream of living and working in the Rhône-Alpes. Throughout it all, she continues to read books in French and watch  French films in order to reach fluency—which she has now achieved on diagnostic tests.

Kerri's first love is sports. She's run five marathons and many half-marathons and 5Ks. She enjoys traveling to new places to hike and ski and scuba dive.

Kerri also continues to enjoy improving her pole-dancing skills.

KERRI WALKER CONTACT INFORMATION

**Instagram:** @fearlesskerri
**Email:** danceradvice7@gmail.com

Made in the USA
Middletown, DE
28 July 2017